BETSY ROSS DIDN'T CREATE THE AMERICAN FLAG

EXPOSING MYTHS ABOUT US SYMBOLS

BY JILL KEPPELER

Gareth Stevens
PUBLISHING

Please visit our website, www.garethstevens.com. For a free color catalog of all our high-quality books, call toll free 1-800-542-2595 or fax 1-877-542-2596.

Cataloging-in-Publication Data

Names: Keppeler, Jill.
Title: Betsy Ross DIdn't Create the American Flag: Exposing Myths About US Symbols / Jill Keppeler.
Description: New York : Gareth Stevens Publishing, 2017. | Series: Exposed! myths about early American history | Includes index.
Identifiers: ISBN 9781482457179 (pbk.) | ISBN 9781482457186 (library bound) | ISBN 9781482458473 (6 pack)
Subjects: LCSH: National monuments–United States–Juvenile literature. | Historic sites–United States–Juvenile literature. | Emblems, National–United States–Juvenile literature. | Signs and symbols–United States–Juvenile literature.
Classification: LCC E159.K47 2017 | DDC 973–dc23

First Edition

Published in 2017 by
Gareth Stevens Publishing
111 East 14th Street, Suite 349
New York, NY 10003

Copyright © 2017 Gareth Stevens Publishing

Designer: Sarah Liddell
Editor: Therese Shea

Photo credits: Cover, p. 1 GraphicaArtis/Contributor/Archive Photos/Getty Images; background texture used throughout IS MODE/Shutterstock.com; ripped newspaper used throughout STILLFX/Shutterstock.com; photo corners used throughout Carolyn Franks/Shutterstock.com; pp. 4, 17 (bison) Eric Isselee/ Shutterstock.com; p. 5 Billion Photos/Shutterstock.com; pp. 6, 9 (Francis Hopkinson) Scewing/ Wikimedia Commons; p. 7 Themadchopper/Wikimedia Commons; p. 9 (flag) Dennis K. Johnson/ Getty Images; p. 11 DcoetzeeBot/Wikimedia Commons; p. 12 f11photo/Shutterstock.com; p. 13 Wehwalt/ Wikimedia Commons; p. 15 (Benjamin Franklin) Stock Montage/Contributor/Archive Photos/Getty Images; p. 15 (Great Seal) Andrew B. Graham/Getty Images; p. 16 Bruce Macqueen/Shutterstock.com; p. 17 (bald eagle) JBKC/Shutterstock.com; p. 19 (Uncle Sam) Bettman/Contributor/Bettman/Getty Images; p. 19 ("Yankee Doodle") MPI/Stringer/Archive Photos/Getty Images; p. 20 Fma12/Wikimedia Commons; p. 21 The New York Historical Society/Contributor/Archive Photos/Getty Images; p. 23 (top) dibrova/ Shutterstock.com; p. 23 (bottom) Thegreenj~commonswiki/Wikimedia Commons; p. 25 Sharp/ Shutterstock.com; p. 26 Claudio Divizia/Shutterstock.com; p. 27 (Statue of Liberty) brunopnogueira86/ Shutterstock.com; p. 27 (Mount Rushmore) Bucchi Francesco/Shutterstock.com; p. 29 (flag) Avenue/ Wikimedia Commons; p. 29 (poem) Spellcast/Wikimedia Commons; p. 29 (map) Armita/Shutterstock.com.

Printed in China

CPSIA compliance information: Batch #CW17GS: For further information contact Gareth Stevens, New York, New York at 1-800-542-2595.

CONTENTS

Words in the glossary appear in **bold** type the first time they are used in the text.

HISTORIC STORIES

When you think about the United States, what's the first thing you picture? Is it a red, white, and blue flag with stars and stripes? Do you think of a proud bald eagle? Both of these are **symbols** of the country.

Sometimes, though, the popular stories we hear about these symbols are false. For example, the person you may think created the US flag probably didn't. And a story often told about the bald eagle isn't true. Read on to find out more!

BALD EAGLE

A RED, WHITE, AND BLUE TALE

In 1776, the colonies that would become the United States were fighting for their freedom from England. One story that has been passed down says that George Washington, soon to be the new country's first president, visited a woman named Betsy Ross with an important question.

Washington, the story goes, asked Ross to sew a flag with 13 stripes and 13 stars. She agreed, sealing her place in history as the creator of the American flag. But is this true?

BETSY ROSS

6

One of the first US flags had 13 stars arranged in a circle. The 13 stars and 13 stripes were symbols of the original 13 colonies.

7

THE MYTH: BETSY ROSS CREATED THE FIRST US FLAG.

THE FACTS:

Many people still learn the Betsy Ross story about the US flag. However, there's no evidence, or proof, that Betsy Ross (who was born Elizabeth Griscom) created the **design.** The myth may have started nearly 100 years later when her grandson told some people the story. For many years after, it was reported as the truth.

Today, however, most historians agree that Ross probably didn't create the first American flag. However, records show she did sew flags at her home in Philadelphia, Pennsylvania.

After its creation, the US flag didn't change again until 1794, when two stripes and two stars were added after Vermont and Kentucky joined the United States.

SO WHO DID?

Many think a man named Francis Hopkinson, one of the signers of the Declaration of Independence, designed the first flag. However, some records report he wasn't the only designer.

FRANCIS HOPKINSON

9

RING OUT FOR LIBERTY

THE LIBERTY BELL RANG ON JULY 4, 1776.

THE FACTS:

July 4, 1776, was the day Congress approved the Declaration of Independence. Many people believe the Liberty Bell rang that day, announcing the colonies' freedom from England. Although this story has been repeated many times, it isn't true. People in Philadelphia didn't celebrate until July 8.

It's also said that the bell may have been rung on July 8 to mark the reading of the Declaration of Independence. However, there's no proof of this story, either.

The Liberty Bell is actually older than the United States!
It was first made in 1752 and recast, or reformed, twice.

SYMBOL OF FREEDOM

The Liberty Bell wasn't actually called by that name until the 1830s, when people used it as a symbol of the fight to end slavery.

11

The crack you see on the Liberty Bell is actually a repair! The Liberty Bell rests today in Independence National Historic Park in Philadelphia, Pennsylvania.

FIXING THE FLAW

Metalworkers widened the crack on the Liberty Bell so the sides wouldn't rub together. They placed rods in the crack. Still, another crack began that ran up through the word "Liberty."

Some people even say the Liberty Bell rang out to celebrate freedom until it cracked. In fact, many stories exist about how the Liberty Bell got its crack. Most believe it cracked in 1835 during the **funeral** of John Marshall, chief justice of the US Supreme Court.

There's one thing we do know: The bell was already cracked in February 1846, when it was rung in honor of George Washington's birthday. That was the last time it was rung.

SECOND LIBERTY BELL CRACK

FOR THE BIRDS

BENJAMIN FRANKLIN WANTED THE TURKEY TO BE A NATIONAL SYMBOL.

THE FACTS:

The bald eagle is a beautiful American bird of prey. Since 1782, its picture has been part of the Great Seal of the United States. The federal, or national, government places the Great Seal on important **documents.**

Benjamin Franklin was one of the men who worked on the design of the Great Seal. Some stories say Franklin wanted the wild turkey to be the symbol of the United States. One reports that he complained to Congress when the eagle was chosen!

E PLURIBUS UNUM

GREAT SEAL

BENJAMIN FRANKLIN

15

As funny as this might sound, the story isn't true. Benjamin Franklin's original design for the seal didn't have a turkey or any bird at all.

However, there's some truth to the tale. In a 1784 letter to his daughter, Franklin said that the eagle in the chosen design looked like a turkey. He went on to write that he didn't like the eagle. He said it was **cowardly**

WILD TURKEY

and lazy for stealing fish from other birds. He admired the wild turkey, which he called "a bird of courage."

WHERE THE BUFFALO ROAM

The eagle isn't the only animal used as a symbol of the United States. In May 2016, the American bison, which is sometimes called the buffalo, was named the national **mammal**.

AMERICAN BISON

The bald eagle is the only eagle native to North America alone.

SAY UNCLE!

"UNCLE SAM" WAS MADE UP FOR RECRUITMENT DURING WORLD WAR I AND WORLD WAR II.

THE FACTS:

Every American knows who Uncle Sam is: He's a white-haired, bearded man dressed in red, white, and blue. This symbol of the United States appeared on posters recruiting soldiers to fight in World War I (1914–1918) and World War II (1939–1945).

However, the origin of Uncle Sam goes back further than that. The song "Yankee Doodle" first appeared in print in the 1750s. "Uncle Sam" appears in one of its lines: "Uncle Sam came there to change/Some pancakes and some onions."

James Montgomery Flagg created this popular image of Uncle Sam in 1916.

"YANKEE DOODLE" SHEET MUSIC

I WANT YOU FOR U.S. ARMY
NEAREST RECRUITING STATION

THAS, UNCLE SAM!

The story that Samuel Wilson was the original Uncle Sam is so popular that Congress honored him in 1961!

Stories also say that the image of Uncle Sam was created during the War of 1812. A businessman named Samuel Wilson supplied meat to US soldiers in that war. The meat was sent in barrels marked with the letters "U.S." Soldiers, the stories say, started joking that the meat was really from "Uncle Sam" Wilson.

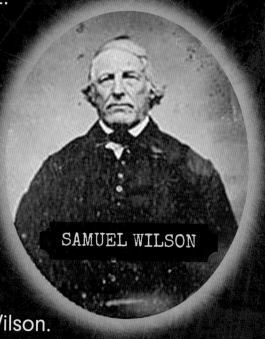

SAMUEL WILSON

Many doubt this is true, though. There's no record of this story until 1842, years after the war. But it makes a good tale!

DC SYMBOLS

THE WHITE HOUSE GOT ITS NAME AFTER IT WAS PAINTED WHITE FOLLOWING THE WAR OF 1812.

THE FACTS:

Located at 1600 Pennsylvania Avenue in Washington, DC, the White House is the home of the US president. Some people think that it got its name because it was painted white after the British burned it during the War of 1812.

It's true that the building burned, but letters prove that it was called the "White House" even before the war. President Theodore Roosevelt officially named the building the White House in 1901.

Construction for the White House began in 1792. In the beginning, it was also called the President's House and later the Executive Mansion.

EARLIEST KNOWN PHOTOGRAPH OF THE WHITE HOUSE, 1846

SPOOKY!

There are many **legends** about ghosts haunting the White House. Stories say these ghosts include a number of former presidents, such as Abraham Lincoln!

23

THE MYTH: PART OF THE WASHINGTON MONUMENT TURNED COLOR AFTER A GREAT FLOOD.

THE FACTS:

Washington, DC, the US capital, has many monuments. One of the most famous is the Washington Monument, which honors George Washington.

About a third of the way up, the stone changes color. Some people think this is because a terrible flood once swept through the city and left its mark on the monument. Actually, it's just because the people who built it had to switch to a different type of stone. The new stone turned color over time.

ABOVE THE REST

The Washington Monument is about 555 feet (169.2 m) high. Another myth is that no building in Washington, DC, is allowed to be taller than it. That's not true, though it is the tallest building.

24

Construction on the Washington Monument began in 1848, stopped in 1854, began again in 1879, and was completed in 1884.

25

MORE SYMBOLS, MORE MYTHS

THE MYTH: SCHOOLCHILDREN SAVED PENNIES TO PAY FOR THE STATUE OF LIBERTY'S PEDESTAL.

THE FACTS:

The Statue of Liberty is a symbol of freedom. From 1892, it welcomed new **immigrants** who came to the United States through New York City.

The statue was first created in France as a symbol of the friendship between the United States and France. However, the money needed for the pedestal's construction came from wealthy Americans, not children.

Some people think the Statue of Liberty was meant to be an antislavery monument. That hasn't been proven or disproven.

NOT A MYTH!

Mount Rushmore in South Dakota was created in the early 20th century to honor several US presidents. The legend that there's a secret room behind the heads is true!

27

CHECK THEM OUT

People spread stories about the symbols of the United States because the tales are sometimes more interesting than the truth. Still, some tales contain a little truth.

The number of myths about US symbols shows us it's important to check what you think is history. The library and official government websites are great sources for the truth. The more you read, the more you'll discover there are many fantastic factual stories about the United States and its symbols!

SYMBOLIC SONG

The US flag is often called the "star-spangled banner," which is also the name of the national anthem. Francis Scott Key first wrote the words as a poem during the War of 1812.

FLAG FROM THE WAR OF 1812

FRANCIS SCOTT KEY'S POEM

SEE SOME SYMBOLS!

MOUNT RUSHMORE
PENNINGTON COUNTY, SD

LIBERTY BELL
PHILADELPHIA, PA

STATUE OF LIBERTY
NEW YORK, NY

WHITE HOUSE
WASHINGTON, DC

THE STAR-SPANGLED BANNER
WASHINGTON, DC

WASHINGTON MONUMENT
WASHINGTON, DC

GLOSSARY

anthem: a song declaring loyalty to a group, cause, or country

cowardly: lacking bravery

design: the pattern or shape of something. Also, to create the pattern or shape of something.

document: a formal piece of writing

emblem: a visible sign of an idea; something that stands for something else

funeral: a ceremony held for a dead person

immigrant: one who comes to a new country to settle there

legend: a story from the past that is believed by many people but cannot be proved to be true

mammal: any warm-blooded animal whose babies drink milk and whose body is covered with hair or fur

pedestal: a base that supports something

recruitment: the act of signing people up to become a part of the military

symbol: something that stands for something else

FOR MORE INFORMATION

BOOKS

Landau, Elaine. *The American Flag*. New York, NY: Children's Press, 2008.

Murray, Robb. *The Washington Monument: Myths, Legends, and Facts*. North Mankato, MN: Capstone Press, 2015.

Pearl, Norman, et al. *Celebrate America: A Guide to America's Greatest Symbols*. Mankato, MN: Picture Window Books, 2010.

WEBSITES

The Liberty Bell
www.nps.gov/inde/learn/historyculture/stories-libertybell.htm
The National Park Service website provides more information about this American symbol, including how it got its famous crack.

US Symbols
jr.brainpop.com/socialstudies/citizenship/ussymbols/
Check out this video about US symbols.

INDEX